Annapolis

MARYLAND
A PHOTOGRAPHIC PORTRAIT

PHOTOGRAPHY BY

Jake McGuire

First published in the United States
of America by:

Twin Lights Publishers, Inc.
8 Hale Street
Rockport, Massachusetts 01966
Telephone: (978) 546-7398
http://www.twinlightspub.com

ISBN-13: 978-1-885435-55-X
ISBN-10: 1-885435-55-X

10 9 8 7 6 5 4 3 2 1

Editorial researched and written by:
Francesca Yates and Duncan Yates

Book design by
SYP Design & Production, Inc.
http://www.sypdesign.com

Printed in China

From its earliest days as a colonial capital city, Annapolis was known as the "Athens of America" due to its cultural activities, a glittering social season, gracious hospitality and intellectual stimulation.

In those days, the harbor waters around the City Dock were so rich with sea life that observers wrote about "oysters stacked ten feet high around the pier." The farms along the fertile tributaries leading to the Bay brought their bumper crops of tobacco, peanuts, and other staples to market in Annapolis. Consequently, Annapolis prospered as a port and major tobacco center for over 100 years.

ANNAPOLIS WALKS A DIFFERENT PATH

However, by the early 1800s, this cosmopolitan city was no longer the bustling port it had once been. Year after year, crops had slowly depleted the once-rich soil of inland farms, forcing growers to move further north. The economic power thus shifted to another port city, Baltimore, leaving Annapolis to walk a different path.

In spite of this shift, Maryland's capital city continued to wield considerable political and social power from its bucolic, by-the-sea setting. In 1845, Annapolis became the home of the new U.S. Naval Academy, precisely because it was a small town with fewer temptations for young cadets.

The economic power shift to Baltimore also allowed Annapolis to grow at a slower pace, free from the wrecking balls of frenzied growth that had destroyed the architectural heritage of so many American cities. Indeed, colonial Annapolis largely remains in tact and is celebrated as the most authentic colonial city in the United States and a perfect place to take a walking tour.

A COLONIAL MUSEUM WITHOUT WALLS

Annapolitans can proudly point to over 1,500 restored historic landmarks from the 18th and 19th centuries and 50 pre-Revolutionary War gems, too, including the homes of four of the 56 signers of the Declaration of Independence.

George Washington, Thomas Jefferson, Benjamin Franklin and other celebrities of colonial America came to Annapolis and stayed at its inns, drank at its taverns, and bought ordinary items from its stores.

In modern-day Annapolis, this historic city of 35,000 people handles the delicate balance between preserving its heritage and protecting its future with consummate style. This "museum without walls" is also enjoying modern-day notoriety as "America's Sailing Capital" where you can find the latest in boating technology under sail and under power in the harbor and the bay.

Welcome to historic Annapolis, a perfect gem on the Great Chesapeake Bay.

Shiplap House Museum
Historic Annapolis Foundation Offices *(opposite)*

Built in 1715, Shiplap House is one of the oldest houses in Annapolis. Its name comes from its siding which was normally found on ships. Shiplap House originally operated as a tavern, an important place where 18th century travelers stayed. Today visitors will find a restored 18th century tavern room on the first floor of this historic building.

Historic District Architecture *(above)*

This is a good example of Annapolis' diversity of 18th-century vernacular houses, or houses that had to use locally available building materials. Vernacular architecture was prevalent until the mid-19th century when railroads began to economically import materials from outside the local area.

Maryland State House *(opposite)*

Built in 1772, this is the oldest state capital building still in use. Its distinctive 113-ft dome is the country's largest wooden dome built without nails. After the Revolutionary War, Annapolis was the nation's first peacetime capital from 1783–84.

U.S.S. Constellation *(top and bottom)*

In 2004, the *U.S.S Constellation* returned to the port of Annapolis for the first time in 111 years for an historic, six-day visit. This "sloop of war" was commissioned in 1855 and was the last all-sail ship built by the United States Navy.

Pride of Baltimore II *(opposite)*

In 1977 on the eve of America's bi-centennial celebration, an open-air shipyard was set up in Baltimore's Inner Harbor to build the first, authentic Baltimore Clipper ship in 150 years. The *Pride of Baltimore I* sailed over 150,000 miles in nine years as Maryland's good-will ambassador, until she was sunk by a freak squall in the Caribbean in 1986. Just two years later, the *Pride of Baltimore II* set sail as a living memorial to its predecessor and continues its mission of good will and ecological education

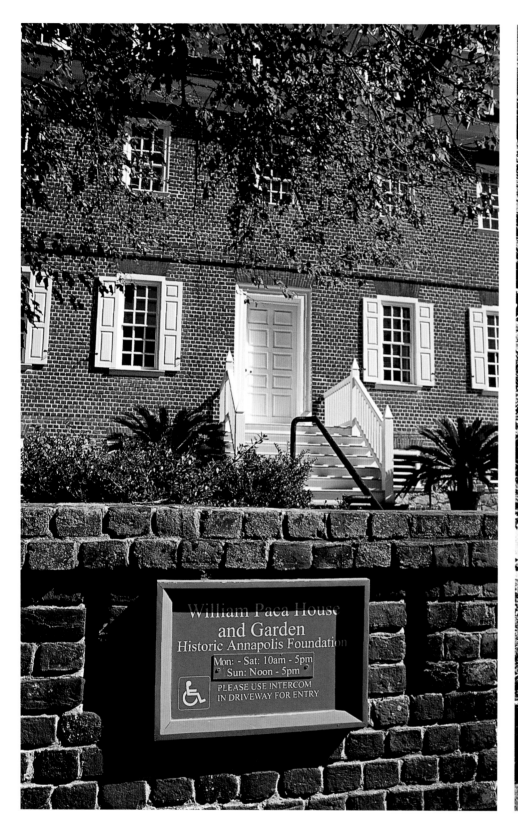

William Paca House & Garden
186 Prince George Street *(above and opposite)*

Constructed in the 1760s, this elegant landmark was home to William Paca, one of the original signers of the Declaration of Independence. The structure is an exceptional example of Georgian architecture and features a two-acre pleasure garden with terraces, inviting flora, and a fish pond. Now a public museum, the house has been restored to its 18th century elegance.

Harry Brown's Restaurant
State Circle

This is one of Annapolis' historic restaurants, popular with both locals and tourists who enjoy the new State Circle Grill Room, a unique wine cellar and a particularly sumptuous Sunday brunch.

The Star Spangled Banner

A modest row house in Annapolis' Historic Landmark District sports a special landmark plaque on the left, front wall and flies a smaller replica of the famous, 15-star American flag that flew over Fort McHenry during a 25-hour unsuccessful bombardment by British ships in the harbor. The next morning, when Francis Scott Key saw that the flag was still flying in "dawn's early light," the lawyer and amateur poet was inspired to write a patriotic poem that became America's national anthem, *The Star Spangled Banner*.

**Annapolis Anne Arundel County
Visitors Center**

The visitors center is a wonderful trip
planning and information resource for
people who are ready to explore
Annapolis, the surrounding Anne
Arundel countryside and over 534 miles
of shoreline.

Flag House Inn
26 Randall Street

Located in a quaint historic landmark neighborhood near the city dock and the Naval Academy, this historic 1870 inn was originally two Victorian townhouses. To welcome guests, the inn flies the flag of their state or country on the front porch.

**The Great Chesapeake Bay Schooner Race
Annapolis to Portsmouth, VA**

Racers are ready at the starting line of this
popular, down-the-bay race held every
October. The timing of the race is perfect
for attracting schooners making their sea-
sonal migration south. The added potential
for hurricane-season weather adds more
spice to the outcome of this Chesapeake
Bay tradition.

Annapolis Yacht Club

There is always something to do on Chesapeake Bay as a member of the Annapolis Yacht Club. Fall and Spring races and major regional events give avid sailors plenty of time on the water to enjoy their favorite sport.

Historic Distric *(top)*

Annapolis' historic district boasts of many 18th and 19th century Georgian-style buildings with brick facades and door-ways emphasized with pilasters and pediments.

Governor Calvert House *(bottom and opposite)*

This historic home was once lived in by two former Maryland governors, both named Calvert. Now it is a tastefully restored Colonial and Victorian Inn. It features the famous Hypocaust, a unique, greenhouse system discovered in the basement of the building.

The Annapolis Inn
Historic District *(above)*

Built circa 1770, The Annapolis Inn is a
classic example of Georgian and Greek
Revival architecture. The stately living
room and dining room are crowned with
their original, gilded rosette moldings.
Large chandeliers of imported Austrian
crystal, marble fireplaces, tapestries,
paintings, sculptures and antique furnishings complete the aristocratic elegance of
this distinguished inn.

Historic District House
Charles Street *(right)*

Charles Street is a charming area in
downtown Annapolis with historic private
homes interspersed with quaint B&Bs,
shops and restaurants.

Businesses on Main Street *(opposite)*

Before the Revolution, there were fewer
than 1,500 people in Annapolis, yet it was
the center of wealth, culture, and crafts
until the 1770s. Visitors were impressed
with its genteel society and the speed with
which Annapolitans adopted the latest
English fashions.

Dawn on the mouth of the Severn River
(above)

After another magnificent day of sailing, boats drop anchor near the river's mouth as the Chesapeake Bay spreads out to the horizon. Annapolis owes its prosperity as a colonial town in large part to its location on the Severn River, Maryland's "Scenic Capital River."

Thomas Point Light *(opposite)*

Built in 1875, this unusual lighthouse is a national historic landmark and is the oldest surviving screw-pile lighthouse on Chesapeake Bay that is in its original location. Innovative technology suspends the lighthouse above the water by screwing its base into the soft mud of the sea floor, thus preventing the need for a typical underwater masonry foundation.

Annapolis Downtown Historic District

(above, below and opposite)

Annapolis has been welcoming visitors for more than 300 years, and today attracts more than 4 million tourists annually. People travel from all over the country and the world to see America's most authentic colonial city. Walking tours of Annapolis are very popular, because there is so much history on every single block of the Historic Landmark District. Many businesses, shops, taverns, and restaurants are located in landmark buildings. Sidewalk cafés provide perfect places to rest and dine while enjoying a beautiful day in this charming city on the Chesapeake Bay.

Annapolis Downtown & Harbor *(pages 26–27)*

Annapolis, in its cherished position on the Great Chesapeake Bay, has become "America's Sailing Capital," where yachts, sailboats and speedboats cruise the creeks, harbors, river and bay. The nation's largest in-water power boat and sailboat shows draw enthusiasts from many foreign countries each fall, while year-round, world-class racing competitions attract the best sailors in the world.

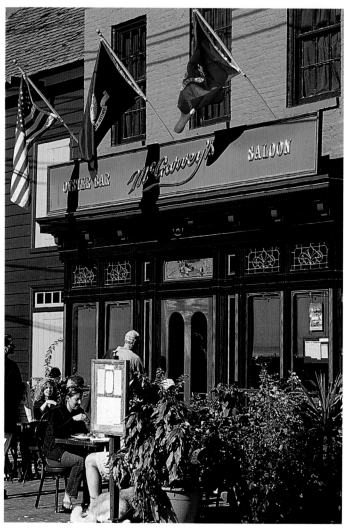

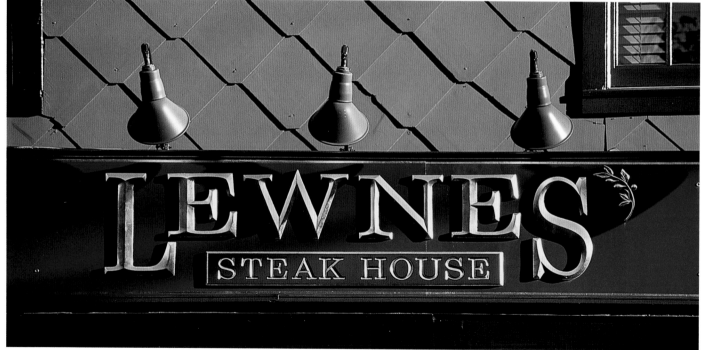

Colorful Downtown Architecture
(top and opposite)

The streets of the city's famous, historic downtown are interlaced with shops, restaurants and private homes from the 18th and 19th centuries, each with its own landmark plaque to show the building's age and architectural style.

Lewnes Steak House *(bottom)*

When you take your first bite of a U.S. prime steak at Lewnes, you will understand what the fuss is all about. Family owned, Lewnes is the first Annapolis restaurant to be ranked #1 in the region by the prestigious Zagat Surveys 2001.

Historic Clapboard Row Houses *(top nd opposite)*

Even though Annapolis is a small city of 35,000, it has the greatest concentration of 18th-century architecture in the country. There are over 1,500 buildings with landmark plaques of different colors that identify different time periods and architectural styles.

Middleton Tavern, Established 1750 *(bottom)*

Surrounded by lush gardens, this historic Revolutionary War-era tavern was one of the early showplaces of Annapolis and a favorite stopping place for famous travelers such as George Washington, Thomas Jefferson and Benjamin Franklin, who used the ferries to cross the Bay.

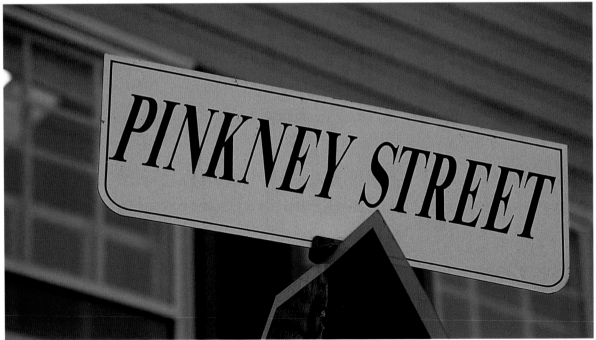

Pinkney Street Historic Homes *(top and bottom)*

This charming street features rare examples of the simple lines of 18th-century vernacular houses, including *Shiplap House* (page 4), the oldest house in Annapolis, and *The Barracks* (page 54), decorated to show Revolutionary War military quarters.

Maryland Avenue Shop *(opposite)*

This is just one of many picturesque downtown shops that beckon tourists with an open door and a room full of nautical collectibles, artwork, historical mementos and gourmet foods.

The Charles Carroll House *(above)*

This is the birthplace and home of Charles Carroll of Carrollton, the only Catholic to sign the Declaration of Independence. Built in 1721–22, it overlooks Spa Creek. Visitors can tour the house, the 18th-century terraced boxwood gardens and a 19th-century wine cellar.

Waterwitch Tower #1 *(right)*

A short distance down East Street, you can see the tower of the former Waterwitch Fire House #1, now converted to residential use.

Brice House *(opposite)*

An excavation in the summer of 1998 revealed cultural artifacts within the foundation of the Brice House that were used in Hoodoo, a popular spiritualism among African-Americans during the 19th century. Red flannel bags (called Mojo bags) were filled with various charms and amulets for safety and good luck.

Holiday Season in Historic Annapolis

(above and opposite)

Annapolis has been called "the most perfect example of a colonial town existing today in America." Surprisingly little has changed since this capital city was laid out in 1695. In fact, Annapolis has the greatest concentration of 18th-century architecture in the United States. Shops and stores occupy many of the city's landmarks. Other buildings, from grand, 18th-century mansions to modest, vernacular houses, are private residences.

Historic District Businesses

(above and opposite)

Amidst over 1,500 restored, historic land-mark buildings in this quaint seaport village, Annapolitans celebrate their rich and colorful heritage every day simply by going about their business as usual. History echoes in centuries-old shops, restaurants, taverns, and even banks, providing an irresistible allure for the millions of tourists who come every year to experience this "museum with-out walls."

Museum Store *(above)*

The Historic Annapolis Foundation's museum store champions the preservation of Annapolis' heritage while the city balances the modern-day decisions that ensure it continues to be a beautiful and economically viable city. All profits from the store go to support this cause.

William Page Bed & Breakfast Inn *(opposite)*

Even though it was home to the Democratic Club for more than 50 years, you don't have to be a democrat to enjoy this quaint B&B. The inn is a gracefully restored 1908 cedar shake shingle home furnished with fine antiques and collectables for Victorian charm.

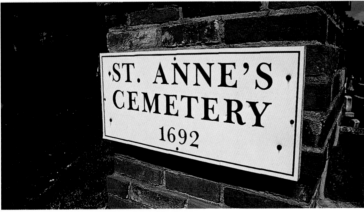

St. Anne's Episcopal Church

The original church dates back to the 1690s
when the Church of England was the established religion. The current sanctuary was
built in 1859 in the Romanesque-Revival
style. Its steeple houses the town clock,
while the sanctuary sparkles with original
Tiffany windows.

Old Treasury Building, State Circle

Built in the 1730's, this is the oldest public building still standing in the State of Maryland. It was originally the offices of the Commissioners for Emitting Bills of Credit, or paper money, which was far more convenient than coins and tobacco, the normal types of currency at the time.

The building reflects the necessary precautions taken to protect the currency and record books—substantial brick walls, barred windows, and a massive wooden door. Now it houses the Research Center for Historic Annapolis Foundation.

Annapolis Yacht Club Race

Colorful spinnakers are filled with
Chesapeake Bay breezes as yacht club
members enjoy the downwind segment
of the race.

Annapolis Yacht Club, Sailing Center

Many life-long sailing enthusiasts can trace their passion back to the first time the wind caught the sail of a little skiff like this.

Donnybrook
Racing on the Chesapeake *(above)*

Much to the dismay of his racing competitors, *Donnybrook*, Jim Muldoon's custom 72-footer, has won the world-class Great Chesapeake Bay Schooner Race four different years.

Severn Sailing Association *(opposite)*

The Severn Sailing Association has a 50-year tradition of promoting a busy schedule of one-design racing events, including a winter frostbiting series for the hard-core racers. The SSA regularly hosts major regional, national and international championship events.

View from Eastport
Sailing Boats

Experiencing this bountiful bay from the
waterline has made it the most popular
boating venue on the East Coast for
boaters who power by sail or by motor.

Even without its sails, this sleek, black-hulled schooner shows all of the promise and anticipation of a future, challenging day of sailing on Chesapeake Bay.

U.S. Powerboat Show *(above)*

Speed comes in all sizes and styles at the
nation's oldest and largest in-water
powerboat show. Boating enthusiasts can
compare and choose from over 400 boats
from the best boat manufacturers in the
world for their next down-the-bay or
around-the-world voyage.

View from Eastport *(opposite)*

Annapolis has deep roots into the very
beginnings of our nation, but what hap-
pens on Chesapeake Bay is thoroughly
modern. Using the latest marine technology, powerboats and sailboats ply the
bay's choppy waters and moody winds.

View from Eastport *(top and bottom)*

Just about everybody in Annapolis (and their pets) finds a way to get out on the water, whether it's an inflatable dinghy, a canoe, or a $100,000 yacht. Annapolis' irresistible harbor on the bay will transform any seasoned landlubber into a mariner.

Ducks at City Dock

A quiet time on the water lanes of Annapolis' City Dock, or "Ego Alley" as it is nicknamed, gives a family of ducks time to enjoy an afternoon swim.

**The Zimmerman House
138 Conduit Street** *(top)*

A rare example of the Queen Anne style with Charles Eastlake influences, this "pattern book" house was built for Charles Zimmerman, bandmaster and choir director of the Naval Academy and composer of "Anchors Aweigh."

The Barracks, 43 Pinkney Street *(bottom)*

This small residence is a good example of the type of quarters that would have been used by American soldiers in the Revolutionary War. It is furnished to depict the life style of the Colonial and Revolutionary period and is open for tours.

Statue of Thrugood Marshall *(opposite)*

A Baltimore native, Marshall was one of the century's foremost leaders in the struggle for equal rights. After law school, he returned to Baltimore and began his long association with the NAACP. In 1967, he became the first African-American to be appointed to the U.S. Supreme Court.

U.S. Naval Academy

A sailboat is moored in front of the U.S. Naval Academy's Recreational Services building.

Classic boat details

Classic wooden boat enthusiasts will tell you that there is something magical about water and sunlight reflecting off varnished mahogany and chrome that can't be duplicated in fiberglass.

Pilot Express Boat, Baltimore Harbor *(top)*

Pilot Express Boats are used in all major ports to take local ship captains, or pilots, out to large, commercial ships that are ready to come into port. Since foreign ship captains may not know the local waterways, these experienced pilots bring the ships safely into Baltimore Harbor.

Pirate Adventures on the Bay *(bottom)*

Come aboard the mighty *Sea Gypsy IV* for a voyage of adventure that children will never forget! While reading a map to find sunken treasure the young pirates use water cannons and discover a secret stash of pirate's grog.

**Chart House Restaurant at Dusk
Eastport**

Within walking distance of historic down-town Annapolis, Chart House offers great, on-the-bay dining with fantastic water-front views of City Dock, the state capitol and the U.S. Naval Academy.

Water Taxi on the Bay
Eastport

Leisurely cruises, a night of dining and
dancing aboard a party boat, or a quick
trip in a water taxi from the City Dock to
a great waterfront restaurant—Annapolis
gives tourists plenty of ways to enjoy
the Bay

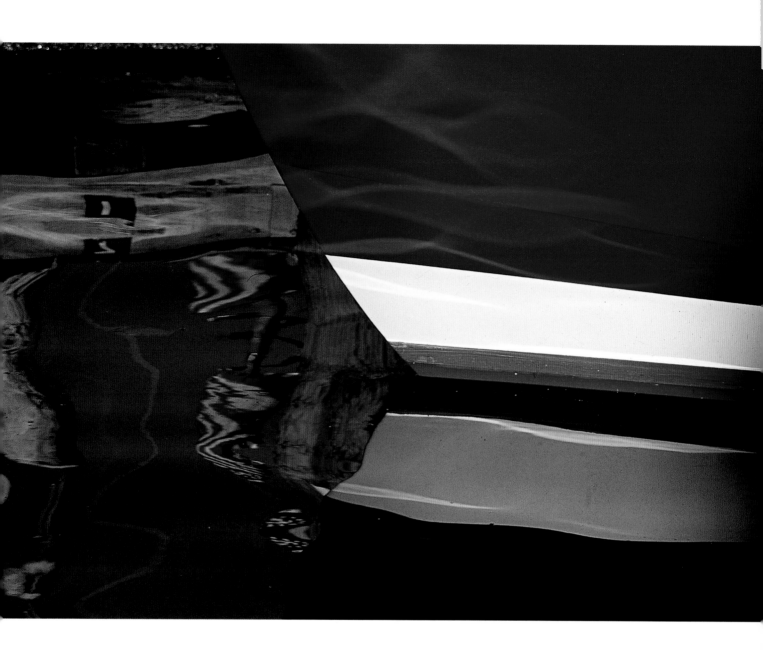

Boat Details

A camera's playful angle transforms a boat's patriotic color palette into a watery work of art.

Eastport Yacht Club *(above)*

Just 20 years young, the Eastport Yacht Club has accomplished a great deal in a short time. Its events—some of the biggest races on the bay—are locally renowned and world famous.

Waterfront Warehouse
4 Pinkney Street *(opposite)*

This is a rare example of the small tobacco warehouses that existed in the 18th and 19th centuries when Annapolis was a major tobacco trading center. The waterways of Chesapeake Bay made it easy to transport crops to England-bound ships.

Waterfront
Warehouse

ca 1800

Kunta Kinte-Alex Hailey Memorial

The Kunta Kinte-Alex Haley Memorial commemorates the place of arrival of Alex Haley's African ancestor, Kunta Kinte, to the New World, as told in his best-selling novel, Roots, and is the only memorial in the United States that commemorates the actual name and place of arrival of an enslaved African.

Kunta Kinte-Alex Hailey Memorial

This sculpture group of Alex Haley reading to children of different ethnic backgrounds portrays Haley's vision for national racial reconciliation and healing and symbolizes, through Kunta Kinte and his descendants, the triumph of the human spirit in very difficult times.

U.S.S. Constellation *(above and right)*

In 2004, the *U.S.S. Constellation* visited
the port of Annapolis for the first time in
111 years. This historic vessel was commissioned in 1855 and was the last all-sail
ship built by the United States Navy.
Today, after the most expensive renova-
tion of any non-Naval wooden ship ($7.5
million), the *Constellation* lies at anchor
in Baltimore's Inner Harbor, where visitors can climb aboard and learn about its
provocative history, including its mission
to disrupt the slave trade, and its latter
role in delivering famine relief supplies
to Ireland.

**The Great Chesapeake Bay Schooner Race
Annapolis to Portsmouth, VA**

In 1990, seven schooners battled their way down the bay, officially reviving the spirit of competition that existed in the 18th century between sleek schooners racing to be the first to reach the bustling ports of Chesapeake Bay with their valuable cargoes of oysters, peanuts, watermelons and other crops. Arriving first in port meant that the ship could demand the highest prices for their goods from eager buyers on the docks. Today this world-famous race attracts schooners from around the world, and the competition gets fiercer every year.

Sailboat on Chesapeake Bay

Sailboat racing is one of the most popular water sports on Chesapeake Bay. It looks like the race crew, above, is just taking a break, but they are actually adding hundreds of pounds of weight to the high side to keep the boat heeled at the perfect angle for maximum speed.

"Ego Alley" *(above)*

"Happy Hour" takes on a nautical theme at Annapolis' city dock. Locals nicknamed it *Ego Alley* because sailboats and motor yachts pull up each evening and vie for coveted happy hour docking space. This regular evening party includes the age-old question, "Who has the biggest boat?"

The Great American Schooner Race *(pages 70–71)*

Schooners gather at the starting line just south of the Bay Bridge. The 127-mile race to ports in Virginia demands superb seamanship as the schooners race through unpredictable, hurricane-season weather and sail through the night in areas of heavy, commercial sea traffic.

Chesapeake Bay Bridge *(opposite)*

With a shore-to-shore length of 4.3 miles, the dual spans of this famous bridge are among the world's longest and most scenic over-water structures. It connects Maryland's Eastern Shore with Baltimore, Annapolis, and Washington, D.C.

Ego Alley *(top)*

Cocktails, anyone? Few places do Happy Hour better than Annapolis' city dock where boaters come to mingle, show off their prize possessions and, of course, see who has the biggest boat of the day.

U.S. Powerboat Show *(bottom)*

Every Autumn, Annapolis hosts the oldest and largest in-water powerboat show in the United States, showcasing luxurious motor yachts, trawlers, high-speed performance boats and offshore fishing machines, to name a few.

Annapolis City Hall
160 Duke of Gloucester Street *(above)*

City Hall is located in an historic building built in the mid 1700's at a time when the only other large building in town was the State House. It originally housed colonial government offices and large ballrooms for public entertainment.

The Hammond-Harwood House
19 Maryland Avenue *(right)*

This Colonial home is outstanding for its Georgian architecture and features a symmetrical garden of English Boxwoods and Southern Magnolias. The house showcases Peale paintings and Shaw furniture.

Art at Sweeney Courthouse
Rowe Boulevard *(opposite)*

Formerly part of Baltimore's 1815 Exchange and Custom House, these Italian marble columns now grace the grounds of Sweeney Courthouse. The columns were one of the dramatic aspects of the custom house, designed by Benjamin Henry Latrobe, architect of the U.S. Capitol Building.

Banneker-Douglass Museum *(above and right)*

Named for Benjamin Banneker and Frederick Douglass, two prominent black Marylanders, the museum showcases artifacts of African-American culture in Maryland. It is a beautiful example of Victorian-Gothic architecture.

Peggy Stuart House *(opposite)*

This stately Georgian house on Hanover Street (circa 1760) was owned by Annapolis merchant Anthony Stewart during the Revolutionary War period. In 1774 Revolutionaries forced him to burn his ship, the Peggy Stewart, when he attempted to land a cargo of tea on which he had paid British taxes. Thomas Stone, one of the 56 signers of the Declaration of Independence, bought the house in 1783. The home is privately owned and not open to the public.

Jonas Green Bed & Breakfast *(top and bottom)*

Dating back to the the turn of the 18th century, this charming B&B is one of Annapolis' two oldest residences and has been continuously occupied by the Jonas Green family. Much of original house survives, including the floors and old cooking fireplace.

Pinkney-Callahan House
Conduit Street *(opposite)*

This historic house has been moved twice from its original location on College Avenue and saved from the wrecking ball. It is an outstanding example of late 18th century Georgian/ Federal style of architecture.

Maynard-Burgess House
163 Duke of Gloucester Street *(left)*

Continually owned by two interrelated African-American families from 1850 to 1980, the house and its residents bore witness to changes in African-American lives that ran from slavery, to the Civil Rights movement, to the present day.

Reynolds Tavern *(right)*

A beautifully restored Tavern, Reynolds reflects the working nature and the elegance of the 18th Century. It is the oldest tavern in Annapolis and one of the oldest in the U.S. It features three luxurious guest rooms and a pub in the cellar that will take you back in time 250 years.

Navy Academy Chapel *(opposite)*

Sitting on the highest point of the campus, the Academy Chapel, known as the "Cathedral of the Navy," is a sparkling jewel of the Annapolis skyline and the centerpiece of architect Ernest Flagg's grand design for the Academy at the turn of the twentieth century.

State House Dome (*above*)

Below the famous state house dome, a full-size replica of the original *Maryland Federalist* commemorative boat is displayed on cut-marble floors etched with ancient fossils. The original 15-foot boat celebrated Maryland's ratification of the new *U.S. Constitution* in 1788.

Naval Academy Chapel (*opposite*)

This magnificent Beaux-Arts chapel is the handiwork of noted American architect, Ernest Flagg. The design embodies classical architectural elements of order, symmetry and proportion via stately columns, curved arches and a dramatic dome.

Maryland State House (*pages 84–85*)

Annapolis was the capital of the new America for one, very significant year, 1783–84. George Washington resigned as commander-in-chief of the Continental Army here, and the Treaty of Paris was ratified by Congress, ending the Revolutionary War.

Roger Brooke Taney Statue
Maryland State House *(above)*

This statue by William Henry Rinehart
pays tribute to Roger Brooke Taney, the
courageous fifth Chief Justice of the
Supreme Court, who stood up to wartime
pressure and challenged President Lincoln
to uphold civil liberties.

Baron Johann de Kalb Statue
Maryland State House *(opposite)*

This Ephraim Keyser sculpture honors
revolutionary war hero Baron Johann de
Kalb. A major general in the French Army,
de Kalb led the Maryland Line at the Battle
of Camden, South Carolina in 1780 and
died three days later from battle wounds.

Government House (Governor's Mansion)

(above and opposite top)

A visit to Government House is a visit to the rich and vibrant past that has made Maryland history so exciting. The original Victorian-style mansion was transformed to the current Georgian-style country house in 1935. Among its many national and international treasures are 18th- and 19th-century paintings by Charles Willson Peale, one of America's foremost portrait painters, and furnishings by Potthast, eminent 19th century Baltimore furniture makers.

The Inn at Horn Point *(bottom)*

Many of the loveliest historic houses in Annapolis are enjoying reincarnations as charming bed and breakfast inns. The Inn at Horn Point welcomes visitors to the warmth of a carefully restored, century-old Victorian house

St. John's College *(above and right)*

Established in 1696 as King William's School, St. John's College is the third oldest institution of higher learning in the country. It is known as the school of great books, because its original curriculum required students to read the 100 greatest books in the world. On this campus, the Sons of Liberty gathered under a great, tulip poplar tree, later nicknamed The Liberty Tree to plan our revolution against British rule.

Historic District Residence *(opposite)*

Stately Georgian-style mansions and houses grace the colonial streets of Annapolis and thrill architecture buffs. Today some of these mid-18th century landmarks are charming B&Bs, while others are private residences.

Annapolis and Chesapeake Bay

Annapolis has deep roots that reach into the very beginnings of our nation, but what goes on out on Chesapeake Bay is thoroughly modern. Powerboats and sailboats ply the bay's choppy waters and moody winds, using the latest marine technology. Experiencing this bountiful bay at the waterline has made it the most popular boating venue on the East Coast for boaters who power by sail or by motor.

Annapolis Streets
Viewed from State House

The narrow streets of Annapolis are lined with a variety of national historic landmark architecture dating back to colonial times. Some houses in Annapolis have been continuously occupied by generations of the same family for 300 years.

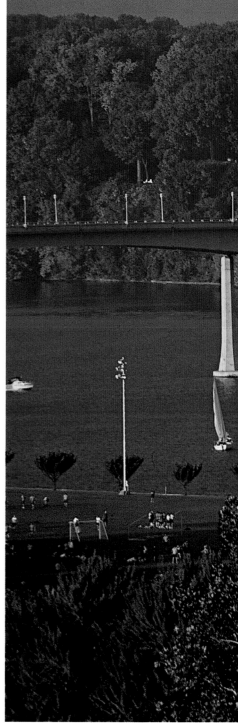

Annapolis Marina

The docks and marinas of Annapolis fan
out like hundreds of fingers pointing out-
ward to the adventures that await on the
Great Chesapeake Bay.

Severn River

In 1649, a group of Puritans, led by William Stone, founded a settlement named Providence on the north shore of the deep-water Severn River. The settlers relocated to a better-protected harbor on the south shore and named it Anne Arundel's Town after the wife of Lord Baltimore. When Maryland's capital was moved there in 1695, the name was changed to Annapolis. Famous for its wealth, cosmopolitan style and charm, the city prospered through the centuries as a vibrant seaport and cultural center.

U.S. Sailboat Show

Locals will tell you that Annapolis is usually an easy-going town, that is, until the invasion of 50,000 avid boating enthusiasts for the oldest and largest in-water sailboat show in the country. A few days later, the fun continues with the popular U.S. Powerboat Show.

U.S. Sailboat Show

This annual October event is a floating showcase on 1.3 miles of docks, featuring 300 of the world's finest sailboats from as far away as Europe, Australia, Asia and South America. On land, the show hosts seminars and exhibits of sailing equipment, smaller boats and accessories.

U.S. Sailboat Show *(top)*

The skies are filled with tall masts and colorful, fluttering ensigns and flags at America's #1 sailboat show. Enthusiasts travel far to attend this show, and many happily travel from far way to buy their first boat or a bigger boat. The Maryland State House rises in background.

Annapolis Yacht Club *(bottom)*

The prestigious Annapolis Yacht Club began quite humbly in 1883 as an informal canoe club on a pile of oyster shells at the foot of Duke of Gloucester Street. Today it is an internationally recognized club with a full roster of sailing regattas and races.

Aerial View of Annapolis

Fleeing religious intolerance in Virginia in 1649, Puritans first settled near the Severn River in the Greenbury Point Area of what is now Annapolis' Historic Landmark District and named it *Providence*. It was later renamed Annapolis in honor of Anne, the future English queen.

Annapolis Yacht Club Sailing Center *(top)*

The 1,400 members of AYC don't have to travel far to trade up to a bigger boat when they shop at the club's sailing center. Sailors will be the first to tell you that sooner or later they get bitten by the "two-foot-itis" bug, better known as an unquenchable desire to own a larger boat.

Business and Pleasure on the Bay *(bottom)*

On any given day, Chesapeake Bay is bustling with marine traffic. Tankers and freighters transport goods port-to-port while recreational sailors enjoy the brisk, bay breezes and the challenge of the choppy waters.

Annapolis Yacht Club

Like the ebb and flow of the tides, the historic Annapolis Yacht Club weathered its share of hard times in the first half of the 20th century. By 1936, it was hard to maintain the minimum requirement of 100 members. Today there is a waiting list to join this distinguished 1,400-member club.

Annapolis Yacht Club Annex
Spa Creek

The shorefront of Annapolis is ringed
with thousands of slips for avid boaters
who sail the challenging waters of
Chesapeake Bay.

Annapolis Yacht Club Fall Race

Competing in the fall series can get very
hectic for team members. The right timing of each maneuver and the precise trim
of every sail is critical to winning. Today
the 65-year-old tradition attracts hundreds of club members who love the
sport, win, lose or draw.

Pride of Baltimore II

The *Pride* was originally built as an Inner Harbor attraction, but the City of Baltimore soon realized it could sail far beyond Chesapeake Bay and be Maryland's good-will ambassador to the world. Today it has a regular schedule of exotic ports of call. At home, The *Pride* is available for day and evening sails and social and business events. Under the guidance of its regular crew, visitors can take a turn at the wheel and enjoy the special thrill of a real Baltimore Clipper.

The Return of the "Cradle of Admirals"

The enthusiastic crowds on shore cheered the historic arrival of this famous ship in October, 2004. On deck, naval and marine officers were dressed in 19th century uniforms. Over a century earlier, the 186-foot "sloop of war" served as a training ship for naval academy midshipmen from 1871 to 1893. The ship's vital role in teaching navigation, seamanship, ship management and leadership skills earned the *Constellation* the nickname, "Cradle of Admirals."

U.S. Naval Academy

The Naval Academy was founded in
1845 at Fort Severn, a 10-acre Army post
in Annapolis. The "healthy and secluded
location" of Annapolis was chosen in order
to rescue midshipmen from the temptations and distractions of larger cities.

U.S. Naval Academy

The Academy opened in 1845 with 50 students and seven professors. The limited curriculum included gunnery, mathematics, navigation, chemistry, natural philosophy, English and French. Today the 4,000-qty student body earns four-year degrees in a variety of areas.

Navy Chapel *(opposite)*

The grand Navy Chapel, with its soaring copper dome, is the architectural center-piece of "The Yard", as the academy is called. John Paul Jones, the first American naval hero, is buried in a vault beneath the sanctuary.

Mexican War Midshipmen Monument *(above)*

The Mexican War began one year after the Academy was opened, and over 90 midshipmen volunteered for duty. This obelisk in front of the Chapel is a memorial to the four men who died during that conflict, the first war heroes from the new Academy.

U.S. Naval Academy *(pages 110–111)*

Over the years, graduates of the Academy have distinguished themselves in many professions. They include former president Jimmy Carter, ambassadors, congressmen, cabinet members, Nobel Prize winners, Rhodes Scholars, and 52 astronauts, to name a few.

Mahan Hall
U.S. Naval Academy *(above)*

Academic buildings and dormitories on
campus feature 150 years of architectural
styles from 19th century French Renaissance (above) to 20th century modern.
(opposite).

Michelson Hall *(opposite)*

From its modest beginnings in 1845, the
Academy has become one of the country's
leading universities, offering 18 fields
of study, elective courses and advanced
study and research. Pictured here is the
Departments of Computer Science
and Chemistry.

Tecumseh Statue
U.S. Naval Academy *(above)*

This statue of 19th-century Indian chief
Tecumseh, the famous leader of the
Shawnee tribe, was formerly the warship
Delaware's figurehead. Now a good-luck
"mascot," midshipmen throw pennies at it
for good luck.

Bancroft Hall
U.S. Naval Academy *(opposite)*

"The Yard," as the campus is called, fea-
tures tree-lined brick walks, French
Renaissance and contemporary architec-
ture and scenic vistas of the Chesapeake
Bay. Shown here is the walkway from
Bancroft Hall to Dahlgren Ice Rink.

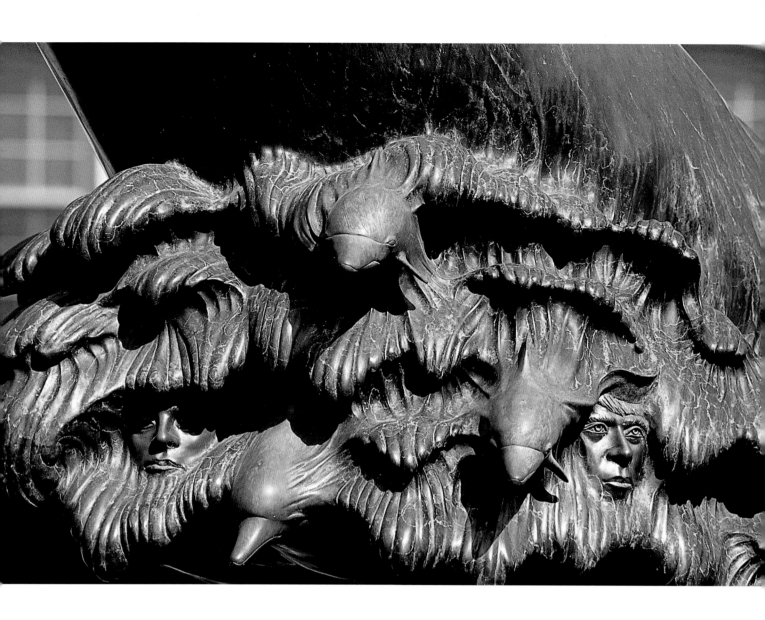

Submarine Commemorative Statue

(above and opposite)

This impressive sculpture of a submarine breaking through the waves, filled with faces of sailors, celebrates 100 years of service. The plaque reads: "Centennial of the United States Navy Submarine Force. Dedicated to Those Who Serve Beneath the Seas, Families and Support Personnel."

Navy Chapel

On the highest point of the campus, the soaring, 200-ft copper dome of the Navy Chapel sets the tone for the Academy. Inside, the elaborate interior of the rose-marble Chapel features stained glass memorials to maritime heroes, several by Tiffany, himself. Beneath the Chapel rests the tomb of military hero John Paul Jones, revered as the "Father of the US Navy." Exquisite, wooden works of art fill the chapel from the pulpit to the pews, and a spectacular organ fills the air with melodious notes.

Wartime Memorials
U.S. Naval Academy

Over a million visitors annually come to the academy, a designated National Historic Site. There are many significant statues, memorials and exhibits of naval warfare on the grounds, such as the torpedoes above and the canon below that adorns the entrance to Bancroft Hall. Popular attractions include the Naval Academy Museum, filled with academy lore, exquisite model ships and mementos of American naval history.

Cadets marching in formation

There are many opportunities for academy visitors to see the midshipmen in various formations and formal dress parades throughout the year. Seen here is a formal dress parade at Worden Field.

Academy Band *(top)*

Midshipmen also have the opportunity to participate in non-sport, extracurricular activities such as performing musical groups (Drum & Bugle Corps, Men's Glee Club, Women's Glee Club, Gospel Choir, and a bagpipe band).

Cheering the Home Team *(bottom)*

Cadets, known as Midshipmen or Mids, raise their hats in salute as their team arrives on the field. Participation in athletics is mandatory, and Midshipmen who are not on an intercollegiate team must participate actively in intramural sports.

Navy Team Mascot

The Academy's mascot, a goat named *Bill*, is dressed in school colors, ready to walk on the field to the cheers of thousands of cadets, families, and locals. Most athletic events are free of charge.

Midshipmen in Action

The Academy's Midshipmen team partici-
pates in the NCAA's Division I-A as an
independent in football and competes
with other academies for the Commander
in Chief's Trophy.

The Calm before the Storm

Captured here is the calm before the
storm of a Navy home game. Midshipmen
also compete in a broad range of non-
NCAA club sports such as rugby, hockey,
and, unofficially, croquet.

Traditional Stadium March

Before every home football game, Midshipmen perform a traditional march from the Academy to the stadium. Every year, more than 10,000 men and women apply to this prestigious academy. Only 1,200 are selected for the freshman class.

The Roar of the Crowd *(above)*

A packed football stadium shows the passion cadets feel about their athletic teams. Upon graduation, these midshipmen will be commissioned officers in the Navy or Marine Corp, with many choosing the military as a career.

Cadets on the March *(opposite)*

In addition to watching the traditional pre-game march to the stadium, academy visitors can also watch the brigade's lunchtime formation, performed weekdays at Noon in front of Bancroft Hall, one of the world's largest dormitories.

Jake McGuire is known for his striking photos of American cities and landscapes. His photos appear in private collections, exhibitions, offices, and are often found in airline and travel magazines. He has won 11 awards for photography and photojournalism. In January of 1989 the Presidential Inaugural Committee commissioned McGuire to produce a signed, limited edition print of the White House. It was signed by the President and Vice President and given to those who performed at the Inaugural Gala. In March of 1992 McGuire received an Arts America grant from the United States Information Agency to give photography lectures in the Persian Gulf Sheikdom of Bahrain. In April of 1997 *LIFE MAGAZINE* selected one of McGuire's photos for the cover of a special edition of *LIFE*. In August of 2004 McGuire joined forces with Twin Lights Publishers to produce a series of colorful photographic journals. Titles that are currently available include, *Washington, D.C.: A Photographic Portrait, Baltimore, MD: A Photographic Portrait*, and *Annapolis, MD: A Photographic Portrait*. He is also working on a book on the coast of New England to be released in the summer of 2006. See more of Jake's work at www.jakemcguire.com.